THIRD QUARTER MOON

Matters of the Heart

Written By:

SHARESE SIMONE

THIRD QUARTER MOON
Matters of the Heart

Written By: Sharese Simone
Edited By: Aaron C. Butler

ISBN: 9781967082520 (Paperback)
ISBN: 9781967082490 (Paperback - Color)
ISBN: 9781967082537 (eBook)

Library of Congress Control Number: 2025915836

BookButler Publishing Company
Upper Marlboro, MD 20774

TheBookButler.com

BookButler Publishing Company titles may be purchased in bulk for educational, business, fundraising or sales promotional use. For information, please email: info@thebookbutler.

ACKNOWLEDGMENTS

I'm grateful for friendships, family-ships, and relationships that prioritize honesty, authenticity, integrity, and genuine love. We get to reveal our scars, lay them down in a safe place, and continue on our path feeling reassured and a little more whole.

These connections are rare and because of them, I am reminded to take pleasure in embracing every phase of my journey – not just the high points, but the shedding, the stillness, the becoming.

Storytelling through Poetry, Prose,
and Verse by Sharese Simone

Table of Contents

Third Quarter Moon 9

I. TAKES A VILLAGE **11**

My PG in the 90s 13

All the Pretty Dresses 15

While On My Journey 16

Red or White? 17

Flowers at My Door 18

II. HOMAGE TO LOVE **19**

Sacred Love 21

Kintsugi 22

Wish We Were Near 23

"Keep Goin'" 25

His Voice 26

III. BID ADIEU **27**

Repelling 28

Lie to Self 29

Well of Love 30

Familiar Allies 31

Narci 33

Casualty 34

Dear Wounded Man 36

Bid Adieu 37

IV. REMEMBERING THE LIGHT **39**

Memories 40

Trails in the Fall 41

Homemade Spaghetti.. 42

Remember the Light 43

V. EXPAND **44**

Tips on Expanding Your Garden 45

Bloom.. 46

I Choose 47

A Moment 48

Letting Go 49

Write On! 50

VI. RENEW **51**

Ruminate 52

In the Garden 53

Tears in Nola's Green, a Journal Entry 54

Little Girl in the Garden...................................... 56

Release 57

Worthy.. 58

Reflection 59

About the Author 63

THIRD QUARTER MOON

The Third Quarter Moon, often called the Last Quarter, is associated with a spiritual symbolism of reflection, reassessment, and release. It's an opportunity to honor oneself in the pursuit of growth and healing by cleansing the mind and body, releasing elements that no longer serve one's highest purpose, resting, and creating space for new ventures, ideas, and memories.

This Moon phase marks the end of a lunar cycle — a quiet threshold before the New Moon, inviting us to embrace this moment as a preparation. A surrender. A welcoming of what's to come.

Like the moon in its final curve, I've learned to honor endings — not with fear, but with softness, anticipation, and gratitude.

I.
TAKES A VILLAGE

My mother spent her final years of pre-retirement traveling between her home in North Carolina and mine. When she came to stay, she brought more than her luggage — she brought peace.

I welcomed her stay, as she was a harmonious addition to our home and much like a second mother to my daughter. She helped her with schoolwork, entertained her in the evenings as I worked or indulged in much-needed rest, and helped her prepare for school in the mornings while I was at work.

My mother stayed with me for two weeks a month, for about two years, and in those years, I discovered the meaning of the African proverb, "It takes a village to raise a child." My mother's presence brought a sense of weightlessness to our home – and the occasional weekend drop-off at my brother's was always counted as a blessing. My village has shown up for me during some of my most challenging times. The fact that I can say, "my village," is worthy of recognition, and enables deep reflection and acknowledgement of all the love and support I've been given throughout the entirety of my life.

MY PG IN THE 90S

Jumpin' out the Arbor View apartment window, shortcuttin' our way to the 7-11 'cross the street. We hung out all summer eve on Brinkley Road, at the entryway of building 201. Sitting on the rotted farm fence, showing off our ghetto tudes, smells of apartment hallways - I smile at the pungent whiff of nostalgia - remembering the brief moments of freedom before pitch blackness. The streetlights must not been working those nights, or maybe the moon held off on our behalf. Peeing in the bush cause the lil white boy said I could. Maybe his daddy ain't teach him the old adage, "What goes on in the house stays in the house." Or maybe he wasn't raised on beatings and secrecy. Either way, I got my ass whooped that day.

We lived off spaghetti and roasted chicken during the week and the weekend eats came free from family's part time jobs at Pigs in a Blanket, Popeyes, Little Caesar's, and Black Eye Peas. Rivertown employed us as we explored the family five-finger discounts, sticky theater floors and seats, Kmart clothes shopping as we sipped on cherry slushies, boring linen store perusing, bank deposits and withdrawals, glass bottled Pepsi and a pack of Newports, "take this ten dollars and fill up on 7."
Black folk, black folk, black folk, we always stuck together.

So many memories of *my* PG in the 90's.

Gotta run down Eastover right quick get some braidin' hair and blue magic for the Friday fry days. Smells of burnt hair filled the air, kitchen necks and sizzled cartilage from my ear... "you betta keep still for I slap the black off ya." Momma was lethal with that hot comb... I was cussin' her ass out in my head tho.

Saturday's morning bacon permeated our home. Eggs cooked in bacon grease with flimsy slices of KRAFT cheese – we were always broke, but never poor. Dad gets the first waffle – tradition was king. Two to three waffles each for bro and me... I always tried to keep up.

Sunday dresses, shiny shoes, dolled up for Sunrise service blues. Sunday afternoons dad's mac & cheese, overcooked green beans, taters and dinner rolls, smell of fried chicken grease embedded in our clothes.

Beggin' to go outside every day playin' hide'n go seek and relay race, baseball with a tennis ball and a pole from the clothesline, back flips off the neighbor's hill, handle bars and no seat havin' bike rides, racing after ice cream trucks, Fort Foote Market five cent candy fill ups, climbing trees and negro knockin', "don't be comin' in and out this house lettin' all my air condition out," water hose drinkin', Mary Mack singin', street car dodgin', double dutch jumpin', hopscotch skippin', dirt pie makin', caterpillar holdin', firefly catchin'... and we never missed a beat.

What y'all know 'bout *my* PG in the 90s?

ALL THE PRETTY DRESSES

Deep purple frills lined with layers of tulle, covered with satin and florals, worn with black tights and shiny sequin shoes. Crimson red A-Line gown with floating velvet black rose prints and a large silk black bowknot, hair adorned with a little red flower. Elegant, Ivory long-sleeved lace with embroidered sequin and a light layer of tulle, white tights and glittery gold shoes

...to name a few.

Auntie D made sure my daughter had an array of opulent gowns perfectly suited for a "Pretty Princess," as she affectionately called herself. They were all pure royalty. Don't know where she found these dresses, but it was clear that her heart found its way to my daughter's closet – and I was a burdened mother who found joy in reliving memories as a little tomboy in pink lace dresses and shiny black shoes whose tights never made it home in one piece.

Auntie D was always loving us with no expectations or strings attached. She just loved as best as she knew how, lining our closets amidst drought seasons – filling our hearts with hope and moments of relief. Her love will always be more than enough for me.

WHILE ON MY JOURNEY

My Uncle D:
He was a quiet and gentle man. He'd read his newspaper while his family scurried about the home, talking, jabbing, fussing, and laughing. Just when you thought he wasn't paying attention, he'd interject, mention something he was reading, or respond to something slick that was said about him through not-so-subtle whispers. He'd randomly and lovingly shout my name, "Shareeeeeese!" I'd chuckle. I still do when I think of it. I always thought he'd done that for no particular reason - just cause - and it always made my troubled heart smile. It added to the warmth I had always felt in their home. In retrospect, I believe he did it to ensure that I knew that he knew that I was there. It was like he knew I needed to be seen, even though I was too young to understand the magnitude of presence and sight.

Vegging out with Auntie C:
Sometimes she'd ask me to retwist her locs and I'd jump at the chance to do it, just to bond with her – even if I didn't really feel like doing it. Sometimes, we'd sit and watch movies all day. We didn't have to talk at all. Just her allowing me to be in her presence was more than enough and somehow, she knew how much I needed that. I'd call her on my way home from work to see what she was up to, and of course to stop by. I'd often bring food from KFC or whatever she wanted. I'd bring food and drinks as an offering of thanks for her unconditional love and kindness towards me – something I hadn't known growing up in my own home. She accepted me, wholeheartedly. She melted my heart.

They were my peace. My breath. My rest.

When they passed, I had to find peace differently - a search, riddled with rolling boulders, concrete walls, avalanches, rushing waters, and miles-long chasms. I endured a great deal of pain on this search, but I inherently knew that what I experienced in their home was still attainable for myself, and it was worth fighting for – wholeness, enoughness, inner peace.

RED OR WHITE?

The parents pass through on their route to Jersey,
Stay a day and wake early for the highway.
Ring goes off - feels like we ain't seen 'em in ages.
We recite our hearty hellos and awkward hugs,
To the room, they put their luggage up,
Mom and me towards the kitchen,
"I got wine! Tried this one on travel and thought you'd like it."
Dry whites and semi-sweet reds leaping out of bags,
Smiles and jolly laughs,
Pours in our glass.
We sit at the long white kitchen table
with our feet on the chairs,
As we catch up and talk smack 'bout the latest affairs.

FLOWERS AT MY DOOR

On February 14, I opened my door to a long white box labeled 1-800 Flowers and a note: "To my beautiful daughter."

For as long as I can remember, my father has made it a point to celebrate me every 14th of February, so this did not come as a surprise. My first piece of jewelry was a Valentine's Day-gifted gold necklace with a mini heart pendant. He declared, "I want to be the first man to give you your first piece of jewelry!" At the time, I was a sporty teenager who didn't value the sentiment as much as I did the necklace, but life has a way of magnifying the heart through all the confusion and unpredictability over time.

Currently, my parents live 300 miles away and we never really know the next time we'll be in connection. What *is* certain, is that every year on the 14th of February, I get the honor of opening the door to a long white box labeled 1-800 Flowers, and a note: "To my beautiful daughter."

An endearing reminder of his heart.

II.

HOMAGE TO LOVE

Love, as merely the "good morning" texts, coffee and antique shop visits, strolls through the nearest towns, eating, sightseeing, and bookstore discovering, is quite charming with undertones of superficiality.

Perhaps, true love is when souls who fervently tend to their own wounds, indulge in discovery and newness, endeavor in curiosity and change, and ground themselves in authenticity and truth. These souls commune with each other and curate a haven of warmth, generosity, freedom, and grace – a refuge for rest and recovery where only truth in love is spoken, where every touch is met with exploration and ease, where depth is embraced and devotion is an unspoken conveyance. Perhaps, love allows us to safely call out our individual pain and collectively repair the scars, tenderly, as an ordinary tradition of belonging and a practice of loving others deeply.

"Today, wherever I go, I will create a peaceful, harmonious, and loving world within my own being."

-Sharese Simone

SACRED LOVE

Like a child
I dream of white petals
and flowy lace garments
angels singing songs of adoration
a solo of strings serenading a symphony
with him I rest my credulous heart
in him safety is my familiar place
for there is no blemish or stain
his kiss is a soothing whisper to my soul
I am granted the privilege to fall
we are sacred
and I am like a child
free for the first time

KINTSUGI

Kintsugi (n.) — The Japanese art of repairing broken pottery with gold. A philosophy that embraces flaws and sees beauty in the mended cracks.

Our eyes met at the depths of the ocean
one could say was breathtaking, mysterious, intense.
The abyss did not evade us.

Yet, we collected our shattered pieces over time,
mindfully dusted the intricate shards with gold,
and refined our being into a beautiful richness.

Our gaze was not of fascination.
It was revolutionary.

WISH WE WERE NEAR

then we'd continue to write our story
from a space that was once wildly ablaze
to an alignment coming to pass.
As we gently dredge through our fears,
we escape the whispers that urge us
to leave our past behind.

We carve our own path
unsure of what's to come,
choosing freedom, independently
learning, listening, reading, introspecting,
you and I apart, tangled in despair.
These wretched feelings,
I know you're still there.

You showed yourself in my memories
of purple bracelet hidden beneath the nightstand
black dress red lips
antique earrings after argument
Dick Gregory and dinner
clinking silverware for two
Oh, how I remember you.

Fantasizing our arrival home
memories of living room floor
candles, heels, shower, sucking
wine pouring, music flowing,
shared energies transcending time
deep conversations penetrating minds.

The imprint of you
I could never escape
no sense of it to make
most days I'm unequivocally
sure we ain't,
but there has never been
an *us* quite like this
forced to contemplate.

These memories live in me
they hold a special place
ain't none like *us* like *we*.
We battle, cry, try, we fail
we love, *we* stick, together "*we* fit."

"KEEP GOIN'"

"Ayo! Keep goin!"

When it came to achieving a goal
He always spoke as if anything was possible.
Like there were no boundaries, no ceilings.
These words marked a pivotal moment in my life
They often come to mind when I feel like giving up.
A lasting reminder to keep fighting for what I desire.
A contemplative reminder of how he once loved.

HIS VOICE

was like reverent silence in a rushing storm,
a calming stillness, gentle wade on an ocean shore.
We were friends with a shared fascination
for long walks and conceptual conversations.
But for me it was the sound of his sultry "hello"
mellowing my uncertainties, making home in my soul.
It was white noise to my REM,
a trancing hum of a ceiling fan,
a warming sensation of a first sip,
like daydreaming of a long-awaited first kiss.

I'd gather many questions
just to hear him speak
rhythms of elegance.
Like prayer as Communion
touched my lips.
He'd caress my ear
with subtle mentions
of adoration, admiration.
"Invaluable," he said.
My friendship was invaluable to him.

His stature: broad shouldered, tall
gently spoken man
with an audacious vernacular
that just so happened
to soothe the slightest fractures
of my mind.
His voice was one of a kind.

And I... I was under his spell.

III.

BID ADIEU

"I am learning to love the sound of my feet walking away from things that aren't meant for me."

-A.G.

REPELLING

Earth   shook
  Broke   ground
You're   up
     I'm   over
You're   high
I'm   left
     You're   in
I 'm   under

From   earth   sprout   new
  To self   soon arrive
Souls align   old thoughts
Shoulda never   new thoughts
  Our story   strange wonder
Wondering minds no   more
 Like magnets   she described
  Reverse   polarity   more   like
Hard   lessons   mirrors   teach
Learned lessons this   time

 Long chapter
Ten   years
Closed   chapter
Healing heart
Healed heart
Life gift
Celebrate
What be
Be

LIE TO SELF

She told him of her issues with trust
how it taught her that people say
and do what's in their own interest
without considering the costs

He assured her of his honor and
devotion to their love
as he struggled to memorize
the various lies he had already told

Lies that patiently reared their heads
spun his recollections
into webbed detours and landed
at a cantankerous impasse

He lied to himself so long
that he was inherently
strangers with
his own truth

To him, I bid adieu.

WELL OF LOVE

If you are not ready for love
you will create chaos

and complain of the rubble

FAMILIAR ALLIES

He poisoned her with his charm, stature and melodies.
He rhymed and wrote, words, he wrote
until she was breathless and knew nothing more
than the lies that spilled from his lips,
disguised as his truth.
He was always available to *slide* through.

His tongue would devour her soft plush lips,
trace her vulva with slow intentional strokes,
sucking her like a cherry flavored jolly rancher.
Her limbs would quiver from her toes to her crown.
His hips knew her every nook and core.
He was attentive to her moans,
knew when to suspend his thrust and when to resume.
His eyes followed hers with each deliberate penetration,
scanned her body as she arched her torso.
He gave them permission to release
and they were all much obliged.

He longed for her and she received him with haste.
He loved her as long as she remained in that specially
decorated box he curated for her long ago.
The box, adorned with vintage earrings,
opulent pendants, and bold purple butterflies,
containing letters of distant happy memories,
was all he had the capacity to perceive.

Safety was not his strength.
He'd *run* at the mention of inconvenient emotions,
King of the 200-yard dash.
She stayed, bandaged her wounds, embraced hope,
smiled, and censored her feelings for an olive branch
and a long-stemmed rose.

He grimaced at boundaries
and didn't care much for mirrors.
He only knew facades, secrets, lies, manipulation.

Thrived in unchallenged freedom
and external validation.
Injections of passed on poisons between her thighs,
numerous times and no real remorse,
just constant rejections of his own reflection.
He'd *hide* from himself, his wounds,
and his constant inflictions of pain,
finding comfort in his most familiar place,
his escape from shame.

He was erratic.
Anger filled his cup.
He loved her,
yet he knew he did not deserve her love,
so, he found solace in resentment and blame.
Her tolerance waned, feelings rooted in pain,
latent contempt and unsolicited unforgiveness.
He became loyal to resistance.
He loved her, yet he could only hear her as noise,
a disruption of his old comforts, deafened
by his own ego and feelings of inadequacy,
voids she could never fill, even though she tried.
He enforced his denial.

He ignored his destructive disposition,
devoted himself to his most familiar allies –
Slide, Run, and Hide.
They were sure to keep him warm at night.

NARCI

Must grab hold of this thing
Mold it into my perfection
Though, it is hard to grip
It cannot survive without my hands

It wrestles fiercely
This thing I must protect
It does not give praise
nor bend to my will

It does not give thanks
I am nothing
I am everything
It is nothing

These beautiful hands
It must admire, as I do
I am everything
It is nothing

CASUALTY

I once loved a man who presented
himself as whole and beautiful.
He'd play the long game, as he called it,
with patience, calculation, and observation
and took pleasure in longingly gazing into
my eyes as they grew rosy and opaque.

Tired of the chase and woes of accountability,
he'd carefully remove the clip
from his hand grenade
quietly place it under my bed
and drive off with his beloved music on blast
head out the window
as the whipping wind blew away
all sense of guilt, shame, and responsibility.

He'd make way to his familiar hiding place,
douse himself with still water,
scrub clean with peppermint Bronner's,
and oil his deepest unhealed wounds
with the finest, all-natural shea,
coating his stench with lavender and mint,
so his friends were none the wiser.

I'd quietly clean the debris,
piece together parts of my body
that were left to die,
seal them with gorilla glue,
and paint over my crooked lines
with an array of vibrant colors.

He'd artfully re-emerge
with love in his eyes,
confessions emitting from his soul
and promises pouring from his lips.

I'd neglect my crooked lines
and vibrant colors, *again*,
accept him with open arms,
and treat us like a work of art
to be tried and refurbished.

He'd tuck his grenades under
a locked floorboard covered with
plush fabric and beautiful camouflage
while keeping the key close to his belt,
in case I attempted to spread my wings,
or
crawl out of his wounded box.

He'd promise himself
to never tell a soul
of the massacres he caused
and left behind
while bearing his
self-inflicted wounds
to the world
as if he were the casualty.

DEAR WOUNDED MAN

How much harder must she *love* for you to start healing the boyish wounds you buried below your belly, nurturing him with skim milk and contaminated rubber, using him to fill voids, pass time, collect and disseminate unfamiliar diseases, submitting to immediate gratification at the expense of integrity and honor.

How much harder must she *love* for you to understand that to cherish her is not to be weak or emasculated, rather it is experiences of rare gold, unscathed diamond mounds in the sands of Motherland, honor to Nature, sacred curation of limestone, granite, basalt, and mortar, building foundations that withstand the test of time. It is the birthplace of healed black nations building businesses, new cultures and traditions, loving homes rich with land, food, clean water, warm hearts, welcoming embraces, and listening ears.

How much harder must she *love* for you to embrace the inconvenience of sacrifice and selflessness, the plight of her who never had the choice and yet she endured bloodied knees, cracked hands, aching hearts, calloused feet, and tiresome resilience from generations of undeserved attacks, shoulders that carried the weight of the home, weight of the man's weight of the world, weight of her own lost dreams and identity.

She only wants to love you, but no longer at the cost of her own thousand deaths by the hand of another wounded man.

BID ADIEU

Hey you!
You, in the corner with your oversized shoes
And flaring colorful suit.
Does that big shiny nose squeak too?

I hear you tap, tap, tapping your way
Into the flowery grave of their fickle hearts.
Tell me, when did you first start
This impenetrable art of fuckery?

I mean. I'm just sayin'.
Didn't you get the memo
That their soiree was a pompous affair?
Or did they forget your name?

Your name!
Or did *you* forget your name?
Trouble finding your mind
Under all that sublime fiber?

I remember her.
She found her way
River-dancing to the beat of
unacquainted rhymes and rhythms

Shaking her ass for the one's
Who could only *see* her
Under bright lights
And whirling stars.

She was *the* star
Just didn't know it,
Yet!
And I won't let her forget!

You are
The light in dim quarters,
Brightness edging the corners
Of illusions lurking after sundown.

You are rainfall's celestial
Quenching of Forest limbs
More than a
Modest glimpse

Much more than a whim
You are
Intrinsically rare
Baby, I declare

Your magic surreal.
Though they refuse to tell
Of your bizarre existence
They just gon' have to miss this

Cause you are burning bush
Unconsumed by the flames
Exodus of all mundane
You are...

The Revival...

And to her shadow, together,
We shall bid adieu.

IV.
REMEMBERING THE LIGHT

"Enjoy the little things, for one day you may look back and realize they were the big things."

- Robert Brault

MEMORIES

I captured the look in your eyes
after we embraced today.

Replayed it in my head
so it wouldn't fade away.

Lord knows I wanted to kiss you.

TRAILS IN THE FALL

I remember us. How our conversations effortlessly swayed from one thought to the next as we walked the Bensville trail. We surrendered to the clean, open air and spoke whatever was on our minds. Nature's fragrance seemed to incite the cleverest ideas and most amusing tales. Remember when we chased the falling leaves? That was a special day. Six miles of watching the leaves float from the trees and into our hands, as we engaged in gentle banter and brief, tender glances. Some memories never fade away. That day we hugged the gravel, laughing 'til our bellies ached, joints and limbs screaming in pain, we couldn't bear to end the journey. Our joy would meet every passerby - they'd always smile and catch a glimpse of our light. We were infectious. I think the trails miss us, or maybe the trees held on to the memories of our heart for nature, for connection, for healing. Walks in the Fall, on the Bensville trail, will never be the same for me. I hold those memories close and release what could have been.

HOMEMADE SPAGHETTI

She said the smell of my spaghetti
makes her feel warm inside.
"Nostalgic" was her exact word.

With each clove peeled
I feel a piece of the day
shedding, stripping away.
Smashing cloves with
the bottom of my large red
coffee mug while
taking in generous sips of red wine.
No music today.
Just the sounds of
knives chopping,
peppers sizzling,
can opener humming,
tapping sound of a wine glass
hitting the counter after each sip.
Ground beef, smoked beef sausage
sweet Italian links
gives the sauce a nice savory kick.
Had to chop the onions real thin,
my child is so picky.
I always make my spaghetti
with love.
It hits differently now, knowing that
with every bite,
she senses my heart for her.
And maybe, just maybe,
it'll hold her over until it's her turn.

REMEMBER THE LIGHT

Music is her elixir,
her author of choice
her "she's gotta have it"
her requited habit
like suspended in
esoteric mystery
buoyantly obscure
yet perfectly free.
How love and tunes
nourish her intensity
was always meant to be.

Met God in her music.
offerings of tears
and silence, therapeutic.
turned fear into beauty.
Discovered her glow again
there she go again
becoming her own muse
lighting the fuse
to her epiphany
a full moon's harmonious motif.

Music illuminated
shaded pigment,
creating heavens
in her innocence,
splattered gold
on blue canvases.
Her music makes space
for new colors new streams
echoing her dreams
light bursting through the seam
She remembers.

V.
EXPAND

"You have to decide who you are and force the world to deal with you, not with its idea of you."

-James Baldwin

TIPS ON EXPANDING YOUR GARDEN

1. *Assess the space and plan the layout.*

2. *Kill the grass and prepare the soil.*

3. *Choose plants wisely with consideration for the various seasons.*

4. *Optimize the space by grouping plants that encourage mutual growth and installing fencing or similar barriers to protect from plant-eating animals/rodents.*

5. *Be open to experimenting and trying different methods that work best for your garden. Patience is key – it takes time to see the fruits of your labor.*

6. *Finally, remember to enjoy the process. Gardening takes some hard work and time but is ultimately rewarding.*

BLOOM

We're in a season of bloom.
A time to release the things and people
that left us feeling drained and stagnant.
Pull the weeds from their roots.
Their erratic nature stifled our
creativity and made us forget our colors.
Breathe in the crisp, new air.
Take in the sun.
Drink lots of water and let our stems
emerge from the soil.
This winter was cold and brutal,
but our roots were grounded.
We've prepared for this.
Even the unexpected.
So shed the dead leaves.
Let them go where the wind blows free.
And as we sway in the gentle breeze,
Be mindful of where our seeds are being planted.
For there will always be a next season.

I CHOOSE

Suffering is like

seeking comfort
in the rehearsal of pain
deteriorating the soul
in pursuit of clarity

I choose to suffer no more

A MOMENT

I feel so calm and at peace... and earthy green. 3/15/25

LETTING GO

I watched a small turtle cross the road today.
My first instinct was to put the car in park,
get out and assist it into the woods.
But I chose to pause,
as it seemed to be getting along just fine.
For a brief moment,
my thoughts shifted towards my daughter.
How it's so difficult to let her go sometimes –
give her the freedom to go into the wild
to practice what I've taught her.
To fail and to rise.
To learn grace and forgiveness
from her own mistakes and from others.
To experience heartache
and empowerment from realizing her worth.
To navigate challenges and self-actualization.
My focus quickly returned to the present,
where the small turtle was moving with swift ease.
I gently cheered it on while adhering
to the boundaries of my big metal box
with four doors and four handles.
As it met the blades of grass and sandy debris,
it turned its body towards me,
held its head high, and paused
as if it were relishing the moment
of its personal victory.
I joyfully celebrated the small turtle,
and smiled at it with pride,
drove off in my big metal box
with four doors and four handles,
and whispered to myself,
'Well done, Mother. Well done.'

WRITE ON!

On my writing journey,
I often criticized my own work and
questioned if I should withhold my sentiments.

Standing firm in my truth, I found that
suppressing my thoughts was like
running from my individual humanity; thus,
forfeiting the prospect of self-liberation
and the potential to influence others
wrestling with their own freedom.

Picture me holding my fist to the sky screamin',
"Write on, my bruthas and sistas! Write on!"

VI. RENEW

"Know thyself, or at least keep renewing the acquaintance."

- Robert Brault

RUMINATE

...one day...

the replay...

Will fade...

away......

IN THE GARDEN

sun warming her back
as she massaged the soil
soothed her troubled mind

TEARS IN NOLA'S GREEN, A JOURNAL ENTRY

Journal Entry:

March 15 at 9:40am

"...exactly 9:40 – don't know if that means anything but, yeah...

Set the scene: at Fourth Wall coffee shop in NOLA, sitting in the garden patio behind the shop. I walked here from the hotel, about a five-minute walk. Ordered an Americano with steamed oat milk and a dash of vanilla... divinely delicious! With each sip, noticeable rings of steamed coffee-colored milk residue line the inside of my cup. It's like each ring signifies a moment of pause, each moment I close my eyes to take in the smell of fresh coffee brewing, the sound of whole beans spilling on the cement floor, the breeze gently brushing my face – a generous offer of cooling from the warm stickiness of NOLA – and the amiable chatter of neighboring coffee lovers. There are four rings so far.

This garden is quaint, enclosed with old, tattered brick. Plants and empty ratan plant holders line the brick walls – some plants aren't revivable, it seems, and some are thriving beautifully. I'm sitting next to this gorgeous adult monstera – her largest leaves are reaching out towards me... fifth ring.

So many beautiful green plants, earth, God. They move with the breeze, vigorously, but grounded. They are me. I'm shedding tears... I find myself shedding tears randomly. Shedding. Removal of dead things. There's so much residue on my heart. Sometimes, the removal of dead things, the shedding, happens spontaneously and over time. What a beautiful day to release. I pause to close my eyes and take deep breaths and release my tears. I'm saying goodbye to an old, long, painful story. The beautiful part about this moment is I'm letting the tears flow... in the middle of this coffee shop amidst aaall these people... well, about a handful. Ha. I'm embracing my humanity. My womanhood. My sensitivity. Sharing my heartbreak with the world, with these people, with the monstera and all her green and earthy friends. With every tear, I become freer. Lighter. Took my last sip of coffee... 1, 2, 3, 4, 5, 6, 7 rings... I love these pauses."

LITTLE GIRL IN THE GARDEN

the early birds sing
return a pleasant whisper
we dance in the Spring

RELEASE

I dare you to stand in front of a mirror
Stare into your own eyes
Do not engage your imagination
Embrace the discomfort
Look at *you* in all your fullness
With eyes wide open
Who do you see
What do you see
Do you see beauty
Do you see scars
Do you see pain
Do you see joy
Do you see peace
Do not wipe your tears
Let them fall freely
Let them tickle your cheek
Let them find the crevice of your lips
Let them quench the floor
on which you stand so courageously
See your depth.
See your beauty
Do not abandon

WORTHY

You're worthy

in your brokenness,
when love has mostly ended in pain,
when you need more time to heal,
more affection,
more affirmation,
more reassurance,
when you're moody as fuck
for no apparent reason,
when you're scared to take the risk,
when you're feeling sluggish and unmotivated,
in moments of uncertainty,
when you don't have it all figured out

You're worthy

of safety,
of the fight to stay,
of loving deeply without fear,
of being loved deeply without punishment,
of being accepted as you are,
of being seen as you see yourself,
of being seen as God sees you,
of being resilient
without carrying the burden of pain

You're worthy

of living unhidden and uninhibited
So. Breathe. Release. Live.

REFLECTION

This book is an acknowledgement of the inherent ebb and flow of *the journey*. It is an authentic reflection of the love, peace, and joy I've come to know so well, despite the disappointments and pain introduced by a life *I choose* to live, daily. It is the acknowledgement of the everlasting journey of self-rediscovery, enlightenment, and profound healing.

It is my intention that this book resonates on a reflective level, highlighting the challenges that come with life and love, and the practice of resilience as we encounter pain and disappointment. Resilience. A quality I once resented, solely attributing it to effectively overcoming pain or building walls masquerading as boundaries. As I've evolved, it's become more about building the muscle that allows us to celebrate *every* step towards growth and purpose. It's practicing grace, forgiveness, and acceptance in every aspect of life, especially the moments that feel chaotic, confusing, and triggering.

For me, resilience is about embracing uncertainty with joy and curiosity. In its simplest form, appreciating the uncomfortable sensation of wet grass on my bare feet, the excitement of a budding plant that finally comes out of hiding after months of waiting, or treasuring my daughter's smile and willful embrace after enduring her teenage moodiness. It's flexible and adaptive.

I'm honored to embark on this momentous exchange as we collectively explore our capacity for introspection, radical acceptance, deep love, self-love, and redemption.

This book was written with a great deal of tender loving care. I hope you enjoyed this walk with me.

Takes a Village

Flowers at my Door

Bid Adieu

Expand

Letting Go

Tears in Nola's Green

Renew

Remembering the Light

Red or White

Homage to Love

Worthy

ABOUT THE AUTHOR

Writer, poet, songwriter, and performer, Sharese Simone, also known as LaLa, was born in Long Island, NY, and raised in various cities of Prince George's County, Maryland. She is a "cool mom" to one daughter, entrepreneur, soul singer, healing work advocate, and forever student of life. Simone has been writing since childhood and has preserved her collection of unpublished works. Third Quarter Moon is her debut publication, written to inspire compassion, self-love, reflection, and empowerment. Her goal is to cultivate and share meaningful experiences with others through vulnerability, authenticity, and intentionality.